ARRIVAL PRESS

LIVING IN THE 70'S AND 80'S

Edited

By

TRUDI RAMM

First published in Great Britain in 1994 by
ARRIVAL PRESS
1 - 2 Wainman Road, Woodston,
Peterborough, PE2 7BU

Foreword

Living in the Seventies and Eighties is a bittersweet anthology of memories from people who remember the Seventies and Eighties. Looking back at life with both seriousness and humour.

If you remember the Seventies and Eighties then you will be able to identify with the poems that fill this book. For those of you who do not remember, this is a collection that will give you a feel for how people lived during these two decades. Would it be safe to say that everyone looks back at parts of their lives and remembers them as the *good old days?*

I think that this book will be enjoyed by both young and old alike. I know I enjoyed compiling it and hope that you get as much insight from *Living in the Seventies and Eighties* as I did.

Trudi Ramm
Editor

Contents

Chaos at Guyhirn - Winter of '76	David T Wicking	1
A Flare for Freedom	David Goldblatt	2
Globe Trotting	Janis Priestley	3
August 16th 1977	Sarah Whitehead	4
The Disco	A B Hughes	5
Freedom	Emma Shaw	6
Fashions and Heatwaves	J Calvert	8
Living in the 1970's	Eileen Bryan-Woods	9
Pop Goes the Seventies	V A Johnson	10
Bitter Sweet Years	Clive Cornwall	11
Year Headlines	Sharon Louise Forsdyke	12
Decibel Seventies	Alf Jones	13
All Change!	Steve Woollard	14
The Long Hot Summer	Mavis Fox	15
Reflecting on the Seventies	Robin Barker	16
Carefree	Hazel m Foster	17
Living in the Seventies	Claude A Knight	18
Seventies Teens	Marina Hargreaves	19
The Shang-A-Lang	Diane P Haslam	20
Life in the Seventies	J Darts	21
Stood on the Rift	David Quick	22
It was Like This . . .	Caroline Shore	23
The Seventies	Rosemary J Povey	24
Plant a Tree for '73	Esme Francis	25
The 70's	Mike J P McManus	26
Lost Hope	Hugh Baxter	27
I Remember	Sharon Langham	28
National Health Service	Jean Carroll	29
The Seventies (Childhood Celebration)	Soman Balan	30
Those Wonder Years	Michael Hartshorne	31
Living in the Seventies	Barbara Colman	32
Gone but Not Forgotten	Erimar MacMillian	33
Bee Gees and Joss Sticks	Tina Gale	34
It was Only Yesterday	Joyce M Hefti-Whitney	35

Time	D A Lowe	36
Scenario of the Seventies	Jim Wilson	37
Smile and Cry	Pat Berkshire	38
Life With the Godfather	Cyril Saunders	40
Flash Backs	Angela Mary Thompson	41
'70's Child	Alyson Faye	42
Life in the Seventies	Eleanor Friston	43
Legs and Co	Angela White	44
The Carers	Alfred Saunders	45
Living in the Seventies	D Pitman	46
What can I Say?	L P Smith-Warren	47
Dancing on a Saturday Night!	S m Ibbotson	48
The Seventies	C Bampton	49
Adios Amigo	Kevin Cooper	50
Sights and Sounds of the '70's	David Dawrant	51
Brighton in the Seventies	Betty Morris	52
These Old TV Programmes	Kevin Fitzgerald	53
Puppy Love in Platform heels	Julie Smith	54
I Remember the Seventies	Lynda Bailey	55
Superannuation	Dorothy Whamond	57
Historic Voyage	Geoff Ricketts	58
Christmas 1982	Milly Blane	59
Thro' '85	Norman Whittle	60
Time for the Eighties	Jacqui Fairley	62
Goodbye to the Eighties	Carl Deighton	63
Ruined	Grant Imlach	64
The World Dies on My Say - So	Gareth Lewis	65
Last Glass of Wine	David Bridgwater	66
Epitaph of a City	Colin Mills	67
Whatever Happened to Global Warming?	Pauline Brennan	69
Refugees From the Sixties	Gladys Birmingham	70
Where Now - in the Eighties?	Gertrude Parsons	71

After Hillsborough	Jean Carroll	72
The Grabbing 1980's	David Dawrant	73
Silver Wedding	Jean Stewart	74
North East 1988	Doreen Dean	75
Of Mary Poppins and Toffee Apples	Emma Brockes	76
Dirt and Dust	Julie Mears	77
Happy Days	Jean Boon	78
World in Action	Bruce W Duthie	79
The Changes in Time	Diane Higgins	80
Radio Days	Darren Powell	81
Living My Teens in the Eighties	Eve Chapman	82
A Band Aid Made it Better	Jan Ferrierr	83
Living in the Eighties	Denise Frost	84
Death Cry of a Decade	Simone Eade	85

Chaos at Guyhirn - Winter of '76

The snow came quite early that year,
directly from Russia I hear.
Blessed great flakes came tumbling down,
we wished we could go back to town.
The first time that we had a power cut,
It was quite late on the Monday night.
It's not so very easy you know,
grading your eggs just by candlelight.
The wife tried to use an old wood stove,
attempting to cook us a few chops.
A wee mouse came out from the oven,
so we chased it with brooms and mops.
The mouse I'm afraid passed away,
my dear wife was declared the winner.
But when she got back to the kitchen,
our old dog had eaten the dinner.
We shovelled to clear up a pathway,
in the best way that we were able.
As we went out to feed the pony,
she'd kicked down the door of her stable.
The paper boy never came at all,
or the postman who brings out our mail.
We tried to get on with the milking,
but the goat then kicked over the pail.
So to all those who wish for a change,
and would like to move out to the fens.
Think it over most carefully please,
then stay where you are with your friends.

David T Wicking

A Flare for Freedom

Launched into a life of ease
Hedonistic needs satisfied
Free love and fun for all
Political ideals were the day's call
Free from all constraints and lies
A generation that in its clarity defied
The pain and anguish of decades before
This was going to be the time, to say goodbye to war
To breathe fresh air and before we ecologically tutted our care
We blindly followed Nixon's image, of a world united without fear
On an oil starved bandwagon, we shed our first corrupted tear
Rebellion of an old age that had passed
Carving the fine edges of a new cast
Forcing an honest future that society could embrace
Without hatred of creed and race
Musical sounds got louder in their moralistic tone
Generations gap got wider in their relative moan
Years grew battles of sex and age
Ideals fought tradition in their impregnable cage
Vietnam sucked in and plucked the innocent young
Transposing a life of purity and peace
The world was now set on stun
Where ideals met blood
Generations got their fix
Reality was the flood
Suffocating the 70's child like kicks

David Goldblatt

Globe Trotting

The seventies slipped over me,
And with them slipped my youth,
From maidenhood to motherhood
With children standing proof.

That decade was so exciting
We jay-hopped round the world
Away from England's cloudy land -
To those where sunlight swirled.

In Zambia we fell in love
With Afric's mystic form.
Its enigmatic beauty,
Its sunsets and its dawn.

In Cyprus, citadels and castles
Topped every craggy ridge
And handsome youths serenaded us
On our honeymooning bliss.

Israel taught humility
How strong the power of pride,
The price of war is writ in blood,
As countless eyes have cried.

In Greece the antiquities
Enthralled, amazed, inspired.
Legendary myths of ancient Gods
Imaginations fired.

At last returned to Britain's shores
Where family ties were strong,
We knew, however far we journeyed,
It's to England we belong.

Janis Priestley

August 16th 1977

His jet black hair
And delightful smile
With flamboyant outfits
Reflecting the teddy style

His fans full of glow
So inspired with his ways
The music was just fabulous
Rock and roll was the craze

Only young at forty two
Found dead at Tennessey
Tears pouring from the eyes
Fans shocked with great pity

No King of rock and roll
A shock to the music world
A sudden sadness and blow
Rumours slowly told

So Elvis was gone
But memories will stay
Of the outstanding performer
Remembered in every way

Sarah Whitehead

The Disco

I wonder, can I pull the birds
    like I used to do?
I know I'm, *wearing glasses now*
    that's nothing, so are you.
My hair's still wavy but not so thick,
    it's gone back at the sides.
It's greyer now, alright, *it's white*.
    that comes as no surprise.
My teeth look good, I know, *they're false*,
    but who would look at that
I'm tall and slim, I know I'm *plump*.
    you couldn't call it fat.
Those styles are coming back again,
    kipper ties and flares.
My platform soles still look a treat,
    anyway, who cares?
I could go down to the *Disco*,
    and wave my arms about.
I'd have a bird for every dance,
    what do you mean, *pass out*?
I know my line of patter,
    would leave the birds gobsmacked.
They'd think that I was wonderful,
    what do you mean I'm, *cracked*?
I'll press my suit and clean my shoes,
    then stroll down *Disco* way.
I hope it's not in the middle of the week
    'cos that's my pension day.

A B Hughes

Freedom

Bored young housewife
Children starting school
Wants to get a part time job
Determined to break the rule.

Looking through the ads.
Not a lot to choose
Couldn't swap one boring day
For one selling boring shoes.

Fancy something different
Maybe a career
Discusses it with husband
Who pretends not to hear.

What about a nurse
Help to heal the sick
It's a lovely uniform
Very smart and chic.

First day on the ward
As important as the Matron
Hair piled high but neat
Oh the aching feet.

Rushing to and from school
No help to cook the tea
Husband very sulky
Declaring, don't ask me.

Doesn't need the hassle
Learning how to cope
Realises very soon
Husband's just a joke
Kids and job come first
No prospects to remarry.

Emma Shaw

Fashions and Heatwaves

How we laugh at our *seventies* photo's.
An age of different fashions to wear,
There were folk in their copies of Afghans
With beaded bands pressed close to their hair.

Oh, those youths in their colourful flared trousers
Platform boots and shoulder length curls.
Sometimes it was a problem to fathom,
Which were the boys, which were the girls?

The skirts couldn't have risen much higher
They were as brief as brief as could be,
Even I bought some cute mini-dresses
But realised they were not really me.

I got out my needles and cottons
Knowing exactly what I must do,
When they were lengthened by only two inches
Their matching knickers were hidden from view.

I remember two really hot summers
When crops were shrivelled away in the ground,
Trees had their root systems damaged
As the sun blazed and blazed on down.

Sales of lager and beer hit the ceiling,
With lollies and ice cream too,
As the thirsty sweltering nation
Did what we British do.

People raced to the coast, every weekend,
When cooling breezes blew in from the sea.
For a few balmy months of this troublesome age
Folk seemed as happy as people could be.

J Calvert

Living in the 1970's

In the seventies, my children were quite young!
One was four, one was ten and one was twelve years old.
Comprehensive Education hadn't yet come!
One went to grammar school, one to junior school
And one to playschool, accompanied by me.

We *watched with mother*
Bill and Ben, the flowerpot men,
Andy Pandy came out to play,
Whilst the Firemen of Trumpton and
Creatures of the Riverbank, held their sway!

The fashion scene erupted
With the mini-midi-maxi look,
Platform shoes giving way to wedges,
Hot-pants and skinny rib sweaters
And wide trousers, known as *flairs.*

Swinging Britain, still top in fashion and *Pop*,
With lots of British Groups at the top.
Pop Concerts became synonymous with massive crowds,
Flower Power long hair and drug taking.
The language of the scene was *Lets make love, not war.*

Anti-war demonstrations,
Ban the Bomb marches and an end to the Vietnam War!
Transcendental meditation, as a means to inner peace.
American soldiers return home to revelations
Of drug taking and, atrocities for investigation!

Still this was a happy time for me;
My children growing up, giving interest to my life!
The sadness of my mother's death, alerted me,
A time to start again, a new career with
New confidence in my own abilities; A time for growing up!

Eileen Bryan-Woods

Pop Goes the Seventies

The Seventies were lots of fun,
With great artists, making number one.
Groups like Slade, T-Rex, The Sweet,
Would get us dancing or tapping our feet.
With the Bay City Rollers, we'd Shang-a-lang,
Wearing tartan, to match their clan.
Rubbettes, Mud and Shawaddy-Waddy,
Even Elvis sang, 'Don't Cry Daddy.'

The Quo, Bee Gees and Jackson Five,
Strummed and strutted, as we came alive.
The Osmonds bought us much romance,
As for Kenny, it was fancy pants.
Sweden gave us Abba with a Eurovision song,
As with many others, we liked to sing along.
Gary Glitter was the leader, tall and mean,
Unlike Freddie Mercury who told us he was Queen.

Yes, we saw many artists come and go,
Like those who had a bit of soul.
The Chilities, Drifters and Real Thing,
Made us sad but happy, know what I mean.
Diana Ross, Hot Chocolate, gave us more choice,
As did the Stylistics, Man, what a high voice.

Many stars I have mentioned,
So many more I have forgotten.
Who's that my memory whispered,
Someone called Johnny Rotten.

V A Johnson

Bitter Sweet Years

The seventies were bitter sweet years
A blend of ups and downs, laughter and tears
Celebration, disappointment, growth and decline
Belonged to so many, and some were mine
Materialism and economics were of the decade
Goods - Goods - Goods, and credit cards displayed
It can't go on it'll have to stop
And the bubble burst - it went pop!

Clive Cornwall

Year Headlines

Second Test Tube Baby Born,
Football Fans Face Terror Gang.
The Vicious Family have Mourned.
Bombs Go Off in Yeovil. Bang!

Charlie Wants Snob Bosses Out,
Back to Work for Dirty Jobs Men.
NUPE Protests With A Shout,
Suddenly Things Look Bright Again.

Ayatollah Khomeini's Back in Town.
VAT Men Row Over 67%
Callaghan In Hawaii Getting Brown.
Carnival Celebrates Beginning Of Lent.

Wales And Scotland Ask For Vote,
Queen Makes First Trip To Gulf States.
More Refugees Come In A Boat.
Government Has Another Major Debate.

Price of Milk Goes Up To 15p
Charlie Opens New Jubilee Line,
Boats Lost in Fastnet Tragedy
All Add Up to 1979.

Sharon Louise Forsdyke

Decibel Seventies

Sheltered seventies, bought tractor with cab
Sort of sissy thing, thought I would never have
Regulations, had forced roll bars in
Next, was cover them with a skin.
Like a violin vibrations from the box
Ear defenders provided, decibels to fox
Ninety seven, was the noise level rule
Cabs warm in winter, summer cool?
Vents and padding all around
Pity you had to step on the ground.
Trouble was, you felt a jerk
If windscreen wiper didn't work.
And it was no good shooting, from the seat
While driving, to fill the pot with meat
Open your door on a windy day
Nearly blow it right away.
Not only upright exhaust, had to watch now
Smash windows and mirrors, on the bough.
Before the seventies, on a lovely scene
Man and tractor, one had been
He rode it, similar to a horse
Fancy jockeys in cabs, on Grand National course.

Alf Jones

All Change!

February nineteen seventy one
was a time of note for all
and change was in the air.
A system finished a new begun
my memory banks recall
a strange recount of fare.

And pennies were dropped throughout the nation
coming to grips with decimalisation.

Conversion charts were all around
some old ones were confused,
surely the government blundered?
Two hundred and forty had made a pound
so many left bemused
that now there was only a hundred

And what a spur it was to inflation
as prices were rounded up in translation.

We lost bob-a-job to *Scout Job Week*,
now suddenly penny was pee
and the grand old half crown was spent.
We put on a shine but lost our mystique
forced from the age of Lsd
and wondering where it all went.

Change had to come but in my calculation
it multiplied costs and divided the nation.

Steve Woollard

The Long Hot Summer

In the long, hot summer of *seventy six*,
when the English weather played its tricks.
Everyone looked well and tanned
as the sun blazed down and seared the land.
Cracked river beds waited in vain
for the splish, splash, splish of much needed rain.
Gardeners carried endless cans
as everyone suffered hosepipe bans.
Grassland scorched in blazing heat,
that burned the stalks bearing golden wheat.
Yes, English weather played rare tricks
In the long, hot summer of *seventy six*.

Mavis Fox

Reflecting on the Seventies

The Olympic Games, the sport of nations
With Palestinian terrorists there was no indication
That they would disrupt and take Israeli lives away
Not knowing the reasons for a fair games play

Political intrigue upsetting for all
Non more so than the trouble with oil
The Sheiks demanding a sky high price
Landing the West in trouble, not very nice

Inflation takes off at a faster pace
Rising prices all over the place
At loggerheads with the miners, Edward Heath has to go
Now the Unions and Miners seek to run the show

A Labour Government elected to put the country right
But will the nation head for an even darker night
Prime Minister Wilson now leading the way
Followed by Callaghan after a two year stay

The Conservatives elect Margaret Thatcher as leader
Strong willed, she feels the country has need of her
Now comes the beginning of a brighter dawn
For this was when real capitalism was born

The end of the decade, beginning the Thatcher years
Reducing some people in the country almost to tears
But in those early days all was set fair
With promises for the future and someone to care

Robin Barker

Carefree

Living in the seventies
Was such a lot of fun,
I feel that in the seventies
My life had just begun!
I loved to wear those platform shoes
They made me walk so tall,
Each step I trod so carefully
For fear that I might fall.

I also loved my flared jeans
They always looked so smart,
Perry Como - sang the songs
That tore at my poor heart,
He sang the song - Impossible
I waved my love goodbye,
And then he sang - I think of you
That's when I'd start to cry.

Labour was in government
Which party should I choose?
I never talked much politics
In case I blew a fuse!
My work was always there for me
And life was comfortable,
I can't forget the seventies
These memories I recall.

Hazel M Foster

Living in the Seventies

We sought it here,
We sought it there,
A place in which to stay,
But could not find one anywhere!
At last we found our first new home,
And we worked in it night and day,
Thinking our roaming was at an end.
Then, all too soon, we ran away!
A thousand miles or more we sped
Not knowing where we would stay.
To sleep and find somewhere to eat
At the end of a very long day!
How that brand new building appealed to me,
Set in a sizeable plot
With some beautiful trees adorning
The garden with its vegetables for the pot!
My hopes were dashed; this was not to be
Where my dreams were to be fulfilled;
Why did those snakes lay their eggs,
In the garden where I wished to build?
Within weeks we were on the move,
My dear lady saw to that,
Down the coast by the Indian Ocean,
We were soon to settle in a flat!
The ocean breeze was wonderful,
The bowling green was nearby,
What else should an elderly couple need?
Something to be sure, for soon we would fly!
A dozen times in those few years, back and forth we drove,
Beneath sunny South Africa's sky!

Claude A Knight

Seventies Teens

At the start of the seventies decade,
Another rebellious teenager was made,
How well I remember those years,
Bringing for me both joy and tears.

The mini-skirts and platform shoes,
Bright tank tops and flared trews,
For a teenager, clothes were a passion,
The greatest follower of every fashion.

Top of the Pops every Thursday night,
In our sitting room, I looked such a sight,
Dancing and singing, pretending to be,
All of those famous pop stars appearing on TV.

Then after all those years of learning,
The government decided to change the sterling,
No longer counting in pounds, shillings and pence,
With decimal coins we had to make some sense.

Towards the end of this formidable decade,
A bond of true love was made,
And for me the wedding bells did ring,
All the congregation did joyfully sing.

Settling into a new kind of life,
I respectfully became a dutiful wife,
Cooking, cleaning and chores to do,
All of this for me was most new.

Then with the summer of 1979,
A little baby girl became mine,
Which brings me back to 1993,
With a teenager, to remind me of me!

Marina Hargreaves

The Shang-A-Lang

Tartan flowers in an urban glen,
woozy on air and oestrogen,
mandolin and guitar-twang,
chasing the chase, the Shang-a-lang.

Curtailed jeans, bumblebee socks,
baseball boots, upright locks . . .
We love you, Les. We want Eric.
Was torture ever this mesmeric?

Sustained by a pocket larder,
smooching the windows of Granada.
Stomping up thunder in Belle Vue.
Tingles too different to construe.

Spending spends on albums, mags,
rosettes, pennants, badges, bags . . .
Swiping streamers off a set.
Bartering tales of almost-met.

Volume controls stuck at max,
we lived that melody, simplistic, lax,
till parents flipped, the neighbours created,
way after the last note had abated.

Diane P Haslam

Life in the Seventies

The seventies was quite a while ago,
Although it doesn't seem like long.
Good music stole the show,
The lyrics were strong,
The Bay City Rollers were the group the
teenagers wanted to hear,
I think this was the best decade for music
that was good.
You could give a cheer,
Just as you thought you should,
People wore tank tops and flowery shirts,
Girls wore poncho's,
And mini-skirts,
The strange shoes the lads chose,
They made them so tall,
They wore two tone trousers,
And made the girls look small,
The boys shaved their heads and
became skinheads
People wore leather jackets.
There were teddy boys and punk rockers,
Some were shockers,
For me it was early to bed.
If you were let,
You could have fun in the seventies,
That certainly could be said.

J Darts

Stood on the Rift

Towards the subway he headed,
wary but worldly,
adorned in satin and sequin,
with pleading strings he touched the parade.
The chorus consoling sailed to our youth.
Our role was to party,
we danced on the dunes.
In our bangles and beads,
we were not always a part of our parents' plan.
We gave our support to the union man.
Stood on the rift, we sprayed glitter in our hair,
we wanted to be glam, we thought we were famous,
but after years of bliss waiting to be crowned,
we were so naive,
just like the last generation, blowing in the wind,
the wind we do age fast.
In despair, we wore studs and pierced ears
and now grew spiky hair.
We wanted to be dangerous.
The wheels of the world we pedalled till dawn,
but there were no mysteries left,
just you, me and the liquor
in a musty old carriage.
So in our faded flares and grandad vests,
we rolled the dice once more.
At twenty this was so much fun,
at thirty only just and I suppose at forty very rare.
The echoes remain, but anchored to the city walls,
the ripples turn and kiss the sun.

David Quick

It was Like This . . .

Who dares
Wear flares?
Platform shoes
Making news.
Waist length hair
On gals and guys,
Long fringes
Hide all eyes.
Charlie's Angels
Starsky and Hutch
Kept us glued
To the box.
Colombo and 007,
A king uncrowned was Mister Fox.
Paul and Ringo . . . still going,
John and Yoko . . . mind blowing!
Creeps in Mrs T.
Bionic Woman!
Leaps in Prince Charles
Action man!
The King is dead
Cry for Elvis
Minders here, T McCann.
Peace and flowers,
Hippie bowers.
Beads, elation
Meditation.
Ban the bomb . . . er annihilation,
Jesus lives . . . our salvation.

Caroline Shore

The Seventies

Now you're in your forties,
You don't feel old.
Life is just beginning,
You're feeling bold.

Working at the Hospital,
Meeting with a friend.
Why not help the patients,
Get them on the mend.

You must do some training,
Now is the time
Do your State Enrolment.
In your prime.

Lots of study taken,
Mother and her sons,
GCE's and tutors
Bedpans by the tons.

Open up your letter
Eager faces shine.
We are pleased to tell you!
The winning line.

Change into your uniform,
Dark green belt.
SEN
Imagine how I felt.

Rosemary J Povey

Plant a Tree for '73

The trees came -
Each a sturdy sapling,
Five hundred stems
Waiting for planting

Each had its guard
Of plastic foil
To deter the rabbits
From burrowing in the soil.

Then the winds came -
Gusting from the sea,
Howling westerlies
Bending each tree.

Then the snows came -
Burying trunk and heath,
And the rains came
To water the roots beneath.

Then the owls came -
And the hawks and doves,
Nesting in the branches
Spreading out above.

And the finches and pipits
Adding colour and song
From copse to copse
All the day long.

Esme Francis

The 70's

Leaving school - feeling cool,
getting a job - earning a few bob.
First week's wage - dad full of praise.
Going out and having a drink,
feeling ill - head in the sink.

Money came and went,
on clothes and records it was spent.
Loud music filling my room,
watching man walking on the moon.
T Rex, Sweet and Slade - by God we had it made.

Young girls would cry and scream,
as they watched their teenybopper dream.
The Osmonds, Rollers and all,
were certainly having a ball.

We knew Glam Rock wouldn't stay,
the Glam Kings had had their day.
Out went glitter, flares and platform boots,
to be replaced by drainpipe trousers and suits.

Heavy music came into the fold,
we listened as we began to get old.
Our hair was long, T shirts and jeans were in.
Listening to loud music wasn't a sin.

We said goodbye to some of our heroes,
Morrison - Hendrix - Joplin. Elvis and Marc Bolan.
But they still live in our minds,
who will we have to remember, when we leave the Nineties behind?
Morrison - Hendrix - Joplin. Elvis - Lennon - Bolan.

Mike J P McManus

Lost Hope

Seventeen years have now gone by
since Harold left the nest
the Common Market will be great
that's what the MP's said
and now the rot is setting in,
and down and down we go,
the mills are closed the coal
mines too, and ships will sail no more
the fishermen are up in arms and
wondering what to do, no one seems to care
no more as unemployment sores,
what's a few more out of work
we will join the queue once more,
we will draw the dole and stay in bed
maybe do a little bit an odd job here
an odd job there it helps the days go
by until the giro day arrives.
What lies ahead no one knows,
but one thing is for sure
the country's going down the drain,
the future is unsure,
the MP's smile and talk a lot
but someone has to pay;
a tax on this a tax on that
we will make the people pay.

Hugh Baxter

I Remember

I remember very clearly
what life was like back
then with platform shoes
purdie hair and fringes all the
rage and music I loved
to hear, I think the best
for me was at the end.

For I fell in love and
married you see and was
awaiting the birth of my
first born to be.
With anticipation and fear the
wait seemed like a year
the longing and wonder was
beyond any words.
To hold it in my arms
got more intense with time.
All good advice came my way
with all good intentions
they scared the hell out of me.
The day had come at last
he was there in my arms
and from that moment on
I knew with all I had
been through he was worth it all
to me for the love I felt
was beyond anything for me.

Sharon Langham

National Health Service

They sat in the doctor's waiting room
And nobody uttered a word,
On the wall a notice said *Silence*
So never a sound could be heard.

The receptionist called the names out
Her mouth was stuffed with a plum,
Even on one of her good days
Life really was never much fun.

'Mum, why has that lady got a fat tummy?'
'Ssh-ssh,' his mother replied,
While the old man in the corner closed his eyes
And everyone thought that he'd died.

'Next patient, please,' the receptionist called,
Whoever it was knew it well,
Mrs Green in a hustle made haste for the door
Glad to be saved by the bell.

'Alright man,' the newcomer said,
As he opened the door to the *pad*
With metal stud belt and helmet to boot
He was obviously *Jack the Lad.*

The boy in the jeans and the black leather jacket
Said, 'Watcher there old mate,
Watcher doin' 'ere, I thought you was sick?'
And the other said, 'No I feel great!'

'Been to a gig and got sick as a pig,
And then I just fell of my bike.'
The receptionist cried, 'You'll all have to wait,
The doctor's just gone off on strike!'

Jean Carroll

The Seventies (Childhood Celebration)

The seventies: decade of my celebration.
The seventies: a childhood celebration.

Making of an individual, a conscience,
Made to make a difference.
The world in no need of comprehension,
Via categorised explanations.
In the realm of childhood,
All illogicalities are understood.

Every memory golden,
Anything incriminating forgotten.
Summers sunny, winters snowy,
Morning grass dewy, few days rainy.

Attending nursery to paint, make, meet friends.
Building castles in warm sand again and again.
Peddling a red car through imaginative worlds,
Journeying to all destinations on Earth.
Playing in parks from dawns to sunsets,
At night, dreaming all this in bed.

The seventies: decade of my creation.
The seventies: my childhood celebration.

Soman Balan

Those Wonder Years

The late seventies we were bored with flares, platform shoes, and
minis, what we needed was an alternative solution,
the monster created eventually turned into a music revolution.
Razor blades, chains, safety pins and vomit became the norm,
whilst fresh, raw and exciting bands took the music world by storm.
Dimly lit cellars and dingy smoke filled rooms, a heaving mass
of bodies, our clothes ripped and torn,
our dance was outrageous the pogo was born.
We wanted to shock they wanted to stare, *disgusting*, they uttered
but we didn't care.
The Stranglers, the Clash, Sex pistols and the Damned were
the groups we went to see play,
a far cry from those nice clean cut boys next door we see today.
Leopard skin trousers, tartan and leather with zips,
ashen faced girls with black painted nails and lips,
yellow, green and blue coloured spiky hair or striped black and white
like a skunk, heads did we turn, those happy, carefree days
when we were punks.

Michael Hartshorne

Living in the Seventies

The seventies was a golden decade
A time I hold so dear
In seventy one I wed in white brocade
And had a son the following year.

It was a double celebration
For Preston held its Guild that year
A *once every twenty years* occasion,
That we Prestonians hold so dear!

A second son followed in seventy four
Could any couple ask for more?
But a little girl was a great surprise
The apple of her daddy's eyes.

Generally life was fun
Until decimalisation begun.
It left us in complete disillusion
No more £ S D just complete confusion!

Barbara Colman

Gone but Not Forgotten

Aberdeen the oil capital began
Americans Americans everywhere
Streets crowded with people you did not know
House prices, food, clothing up and up.
The city is ill parted.
The poor are poorer, rich are richer.
Drugs, muggings, rape are rife
George Street knocked down like the blitz.
Progress they call it.
We the people of Aberdeen call it lost
We lose our way no familiar land marks
One way streets lost again
Parking cars where can we go?
No space left filled in by the new
Cinema's gone bingo bingo everywhere
Docks are full of empty boxes
Where are the fish?
They may have swam away
They do not like the oil I'll say
Now the good things in the seventies
My two grandsons born healthy
Helen's Karl and Pauline's Robert
The apple of their grannie Erimar's eye
Never mind the changes
We love our silver city by the sea
At the mouth of Don and Dee
The can't take that away
Can they?

Erimar MacMillian

Bee Gees and Joss Sticks

Living in the seventies
Although then quite young
I wore lilac hotpants
Despite complaints from mum

I threaded lovebeads
By the score
And hung jingling bells
Outside the door

Joss sticks burned away
Oozing with a choking scent
As I camped out one night
In a small and leaky tent

Bee Gee's music played at parties
And I drank sweet pomagne
Dancing all night in platforms
Before limping home again

A flower powered person
Living for love
I painted peaceful pictures
Depicting white doves

Tina Gale

It was Only Yesterday

It seems like only yesterday we'd all been to San Franciso.
Love was power, had banned the bomb, we'd had flowers in our hair.
Now it's Marc Bolan, T Rex in satin pants and sequinned bolero!
Inviting us to ride his white swan and talk to his metal guru!
Both teenage sons falling in love, pretending not to care,
One has even had a bath, borrowed two quid, especially for her!
Happily he's been jilted, I sigh he's handsome, *don't you worry*,
He'd cried in secret, consoles himself, *she made a rubbish curry!*
Daughter only little, watches *fingermouse*, then Pan's People dance,
She wants to be just like *Cherry*, and mimics her in a trance.
Pungent smells of joss sticks and patchouli permeates the air,
Son has fallen in love again, wears trousers with the widest flair!
Poster stuck with sellotape to bright green ceiling, walls and doors,
Words of love scrawled across *Blondies* lips, *Take me I'm yours*!
Avengers are avenging in black leather thigh boots across the land.
To remove them after filming will take a magic wand,
Young joints gyrate now as they emulate the *King*, Elvis,
Later pretending not to watch the *Wombles*, oh, that aching pelvis!
Dad took them to see Gary Glitter, *Rock On* his band tried to play,
Yes, they could wear their shirts open, but platform boots? no way!
Blue Peter badges they all won, an idea for using bottle tops,
They wore them with nonchalance as they danced to Top of the Pops!
The Carpenters still bring me some peace, Karen sings and Richard plays,
Smiling to myself some twenty years on! *It was only Yesterday.*

Joyce M Hefti-Whitney

Time

The clock is ticking,
the sand is falling,
age is approaching,
for time will not stop,
seconds, minutes, hours are continuous.
Sometimes I wish time would stop,
allow me to get off this fast moving train,
but there is no stop,
I cannot depart from this train,
for this train will always be on time,
but with age comes knowledge,
with knowledge comes age . . .
time will not stop,
for time must stay on time,
day then night must follow,
days, weeks, months are monotonous.
The clock is ticking,
time is going,
the sand is running out,
age is fast approaching
as the train flies past another distant station,
another station, another year . . .
for time will not stop,
years, decades, centuries are successive.
But remember -
with age comes knowledge,
and with knowledge comes age . . .

D A Lowe

Scenario of the Seventies

The seventies opened with style and pace,
America had won the great Moon race,
Viking spacecraft landed on the planet Mars,
We were seeking other life among the Stars.

A fifty pence piece replaced the ten bob note,
Politicians hoped it would increase their vote,
Decimal currency was the aim,
For the Nation it was a crying shame.

Prices increased by the score,
Which helped to make the people poor,
Low pay brought our nursing angels out on strike
The answer was on your bike.

That first North Sea oil pumped ashore,
Could it help poverty among the poor,
Eighteen years old won the right to vote,
Would this bring the young a brighter hope.

Bloody Sunday with its sadness and shame,
Causing countless grief and pain,
People everywhere must learn to unite,
And overcome evil with good and right.

Proud Britain joined the EEC,
To improve the lot of you and me,
A Common Wealth for one and all,
Can we make it work or will it fall.

An Equal Opportunities Act was introduced at last,
Would discrimination against our Ladies be in the past,
Will they receive equal money for their pain,
Could prejudice be out and justice gain.

Jim Wilson

Smile and Cry

Politically much better than the men -
Mrs Thatcher moved to No 10.

The Sex Discrimination Act came about --
Equal pay, too, *Well done,* the women shout.

A decade of Royal dates we remember -
With celebrations for the Queen's silver.

Captain Mark Phillips married our Princess Anne -
Princess Margaret divorced her Armstrong-Jones man.

Earl Mountbatten died - an act of terror -
Duke of Gloucester killed - an air race error.

We flocked to the cinema to see Jaws,
And then again to see the film Star Wars.

King Elvis died, but his records live on -
Graceland's a shrine, but has he really gone?

Bing Crosby crooned his very last hit song -
John Lennon went solo, but not for long.

Watergate led to Nixon resigning -
And the tension was electrifying.

Pope John Paul the 2nd took over the Vatican -
A Pole, charismatic, a very good man!

We didn't win the World Cup, alas, alack -
But Stewart and Hunt were first on the track.

Great Britain became part of the EEC -
The Suez Canal re-opened to ships at sea.

London hit hard by terrorist bombers -
        There seemed to be no end to the horrors.

The 70's made us smile and made us cry -
        About the crying, I ask myself, Why, why?

Will the history books record a good decade -
        Or simply reveal the mistakes we made?

Pat Berkshire

Life With the Godfather

A long, long queue, let's get it right
They say Godfather's showing tonight.
His life methinks was dull and empty
Just like life for some in the Seventies.
Remember then windscreen washer's law
And that ensuing great furore?
The motorists wanted many - soon there was just not any.
But law was good, said that's a shame
No washers on, yes, you're to blame
A fine you'll pay just the same.
Now as we shuffle down picture queue
Let's think of other things we went through.
Oh yes, our Fred wanted a house
A mortgage asked him quick and fast
But building society was short of cash
He'd seen his yearnings crash.
Then there were so many roads
They felt we all need postcodes.
Some thought the nation soft and barmy
We didn't need them in the army.
They'd numbered us from A to Z
My code I couldn't get into my head.
Oh, yes remember that radio broadcast
The contents weren't even forecast.
They spoke of lesbians, homosexuals too
It all came right out of the blue.
We'd not bear that and that's a fact
I hope that producers got the sack.
Great we're nearly in at door
It's Marlon I've been looking for.

Cyril Saunders

Flash Backs

In Nineteen Seventy One
My working life began
In the office where I sat from nine to five
Then on the bus and home
After bubble bath of foam
To the Discotheque where legs could come alive

In Nineteen Seventy Three
I could drink quite legally
Until they called last orders half past ten
Where the Juke Box was the crave
Motown music all the rave
Michael Jackson sang about his pet named *Ben*

In Nineteen Seventy Five
I saw Paul McCartney live
We were in a lift together, just us two
There's a song he used to sing
With his backing band called Wings
As the lift went *Hi hi hi*, my heart did too

In Nineteen Seventy Six
Two swinging Swedish chicks
Their partners making up the group of four
With their accents slightly funny
They sang *Money, Money, Money*,
Fernando, *Dancing Queen* and many more

In Nineteen Seventy Eight
I began to put on weight
Each month in fact, and when it got to nine
It was on one night in June
You're the one I want the tune
I'd remember, from the decade, for all time.

Angela Mary Thompson

'70's Child

Summer's drawl, resonant with
the scents of strawberries,
helter skelter slides
gleaming sands and
sandy sandwiches eaten on
ruffled beach towels;
caravan circles.

Winter's crawl, rumbling through
school assembly halls,
blue-thighed on hockey pitches
high-voiced in choirs and
walnut polished desks, tattooed with
ink scrawl, sharp-edged exam papers;
homework grades.

Alyson Faye

Life in the Seventies

I recall a time in the seventies
When I decided to learn to drive
Husband said, he'd start me off
To make sure others survive
I remember the first words to me,
You may think he spoke kindly!
'Don't forget, a car can kill.'
My spirits flagged, I lost the will,
But think of the things I could do
And surely there'd be lots of fun
I did quite well, or so it seemed
At first on the aerodrome,
So I set my sights on driving home
With some confidence I mean
Almost there, I turned into the lane
When suddenly the postman came
On his bike across my path
He thought it a bit of a laugh,
No damage done, slowly into the garage
But what a strain on my marriage.

Eleanor Friston

Legs and Co

From about Nineteen Seventy Three
The world was a dangerous place to be
For the small child - maybe able to talk,
But having problems trying to walk.
In addition to all the usual cares,
We were the fashion victims - of Flares.
If you yourself had to wear the things
They caused a current on the swings.
They flapped around tenderly adult feet
And obscured your vision when crossing the street.
So, when you ran out of pedestrian routes
You had to look between the spaces in the platform boots.
But the fad's following began to tire
As silhouettes got higher and higher,
We looked up to where we thought the air was clean
Because Punk had exploded and hair was green!

Angela White

The Carers

I went into hospital
Because I was ill,
If it hadn't been for Doctors and Nurses
I would be ill, still.

I had an operation
Came through it OK
Had to take it easy
So they all say.

I thank those Doctors and Nurses,
They always give their all
When they are needed
They always answer the call.

The surgeons do the ops,
Sisters do the minding
And when it comes to bandaging
The nurses do the binding.

I thank them one and all
For what they do,
If you ever need them
They will mend you too.

Alfred Saunders

Living in the Seventies

Three score years and ten gone by
Since nineteen hundred past,
The century where man did fly
And atom bombs made blast.

The planets even walked upon
Has man now in life's race,
With destiny they all all gone
In search yet of God's face.

New religions with the old
Piled high upon time's shelf,
Daily love grows yet more cold
As further man seeks for himself

Seventy the years of man
To him by his God given,
Thirty left if in his plan
By centuries are we driven.

Science as a precious stone
The mother of invention,
At the feet of mars is thrown
War still man's one intention.

The decade as a minute seemed
The manic pace now of life,
Overriding all we dreamed
As grows yet mortal strife.

As the summer was this time
We now to winter travel on,
There to reason and to rhyme
With these years, precious gone.

D Pitman

What can I Say?

About the seventies, what can I say?
Something different every day,
The first female Prime Minster we ever had,
The death of Elvis, oh so sad,
Queen the band made great hits that's for sure,
Saturday Night Fever to dance on the floor,
That dreadful long steelworks strike too,
And in the cinema Soldier Blue,
So many memories of the seventies in my mind do I hold,
Some good, some bad and some really quite bold.

L P Smith-Warren

Dancing on a Saturday Night!

Bell bottomed trousers, lipstick shining bright
Do you wanna be in my gang?
We'll have fun tonight!

Platform shoes, waistcoat tight
We're gonna *Cum on feel the noise*
In the club tonight.

Excitement in our voices, always acting daft
Teenagers of the seventies
All of life a laugh.

Now I'm in my 30's and raving is a hit
Loss of *life is for living*?
No not a bit.

I'll be in the club this Saturday
The boys I'll give a miss
But the dancing is so good it will make up for this.

S M Ibbotson

The Seventies

In seventy one, I got engaged
my heart was bright and happy.
Seventy three was wedding bells, so nervous
and wee bit snappy.
Seventy five a daughter born, so beautiful and gay
Seventy six a deep dark year, my father passed away.
Seventy seven my son was born
helps mend my broken heart.
Seventy eight we moved house and make a brand new start.
The seventies hold for me
main memories of my life
that I shall always treasure being a daughter, mother and wife.

C Bampton

Adios Amigo

(The Ballad of the Duke)

In 1979, John Wayne died
And, with myself, the whole world cried
He was known as The Duke, a legend of the West
Tall in the saddle, one of the best
A giant hero of the screen
The Texan cowboy of our dreams.

It was hard, it was cruel
A time without rules
Men lived by the law of the gun -
And so a legend had begun

On the screen he made the West seem real
And with every magic reel
A hero would unfold
We watched - along with him we rode
In search of El Dorado

He was a Quiet Man, a man of True Grit
A Searcher, A Shootist
Now he's gone and sadly missed

Through my childhood years he seemed to me
As strong and brave as a man could be
When The Duke was gone, though I was grown
It still seemed hard to walk alone.
In 1979, John Wayne died
I remember that the whole world cried.
Adios, Amigo
My friend, my hero.

Kevin Cooper

Sights and Sounds of the '70's

Do you remember the midi and maxi-skirts,
Platform shoes and Ben Sherman shirts,
Tubular Bells and the miner's strike
And Harley Davidson motor bikes,
What about David Bowie, brown curtains,
Spider plants and John Lennon?

Do you remember joss-sticks, Punk Rock,
Free concerts, Pink Floyd, Mr Spock,
Bold wall paper, Captain Beefheart,
Star Wars, Alien and a la carte,
What about Jaws I and II, Planet of the Apes,
Airport 75, Rocky and Selloptape?

Do you remember Led Zeppelin, Free,
Rocky Horror Picture Show and apre-ski,
Post Office strike, Star Trek the motion picture,
Jimmy Saville's long blonde hair, memorabilia,
What about the Beatles and oil crisis 73-74,
Stravinsky died in 71 and the Vietnam War?

Do you remember the blackout, Soldier Blue,
The Rolling Stones and the barbecue,
The Generation Game and the cuddly toy,
Rising Damp, Sid Vicious and Playboy,
The UK acceded as full member to the EEC,
Social change, Hari Krishna and LSD?

Do you remember apartheid, General Amin,
Political unrest and African famine,
Abba and the resignation of Harold Wilson,
Hottest day recorded 32.3c in London,
J R R Tolken died, Jimmy Carter President,
Mariner 9 in orbit around Mars, NASA jubilant.

David Dawrant

Brighton in the Seventies

Come the summer Brighton Station
Welcome half the British nation,
Not to speak of hundreds more
From every foreign clime and shore.
Thousands, too, from near and far
Pour into our town by car;
Students (young and not so young)
Chattering in foreign tongue;
Delegates with cryptic labels
Theatre stars in mink and sables;
Mums, dads, kids and mods and rockers,
Punks (My Stars! They do look shockers.
That bloke's hair is bright vermilion!)
Crowd the cafés, the Pavilion.
Shops are busy, car parks busting,
Pavements jammed with folks all thrusting
Their way past to beach, marina,
'Where's our Vi'let? 'Ave you seen 'er?'
Come the summer, I head West.
At that season Hove is best.
There a haven I can find,
Quiet, select, and so refined.
But when autumn leaves start falling
I can hear my home town calling.
Shuttered cafés, empty bars,
Ghosts that ride the bumper cars,
Saucy postcards none will buy
Move me strangely - Who knows why?
Brighthelmstone, I love thee well,
But in summer thou art hell.

Betty Morris

These Old TV Programmes

Sometimes at night I take delight,
When I remember my family and me,
And all those old programmes we'd watch,
On black and white TV.

Dad liked police stories like Z Cars,
And Dixen of Dock Green,
He also liked The Golden Shot,
And Opportunity Knocks with Hugie Green.

Mum's favourites were the soaps,
Yes she really did like those,
Things like Upstairs and Downstairs,
Paton Place and also Crossroads.

Granny was fond of love stories,
With lots of sloppy kisses,
How she'd chuckle at On The Buses,
But her favourite was Mr and Mrs.

Us kids liked Watch with Mother,
The Woodentops and Bill and Ben were fine,
And how we'd all laugh out hysterically,
At Michael Ben's Potty Time.

Not to mention Wacky Races,
I must have been their greatest fan,
The Clangers how they'd make a funny noise,
And Catweasel now he was a strange man.

Yes those were the programmes of the early seventies,
Yet some are still here today that time hasn't marred,
Like News at Ten, Coronation Street,
And the little girl on the Test Card.

Kevin Fitzgerald

Puppy Love in Platform Heels

I was nine or ten in the Seventies
So didn't get to wear those platform shoes
But I did love Donny Osmond
I'd keep all his cuttings from the news

Mum used to tease me constantly
Said it was puppy love I'd got
What did she know, I thought
Now that I'm older I know what

And what about the clothes
Stripy tank tops and twelve inch flares
What must we have looked like
And did we really care

Then there was Glam rock
With Gary Glitter, Slade and Sweet
My favourite group was Mud
I still dance to *Tiger Feet*

They called us *Teenyboppers*
As *Roller mania* hit our town
And as for those platform shoes
I'm wearing them this time around.

Julie Smith

I Remember the Seventies

I remember the Seventies
Ah yes, I remember them well
I left school, I started work
And in love I fell

I remember the Seventies
Mini skirts and platform shoes
Heels so high and I wondered why
My legs were always bruised

I remember the Seventies
Into bell bottomed loon pants I'd squeeze
Cuffs on shirts six inches wide
And collars down to your knees

I remember the Seventies
Bay City Rollers and *The Sweet*
Gary Glitter in his prime
Had us tapping our feet

I remember the Seventies
A decade of quite bizarre fashion
First meeting my friends and having fun
And feeling the first flowers of passion

I remember the Seventies
And an illness quite severe
Two major operations
And death so very near

I remember the Seventies
Getting engaged and getting wed
I remember when he left me
And all the tears I shed

I remember the ending and I remember the start
I remember the Seventies and my broken heart.

Lynda Bailey

Superannuation

Suddenly it's here, the day, the hour
dreaded and dreamed of; hard to believe
it would arrive, that friends would say
'We envy you - you've all the time
in the world, to do just what you want.'

But there's the rub - when that time comes
what do we want, except more time?
Too much contentment threatens, and
threats too are bus-trips and free seats
at concerts, to fill up the hall,
or weekends at cold West coast hotels,
with supper dances and a string quartet

Better to stay at home, lean on the gate
watching slow dusk creep up the rolling field;
better to help filling the hayracks up
and bolting the doors last thing at night.

All the time in the world but all
is all too little in a world grown small
where days come singly, each a door
we must go through
with gratitude
and never ask
'How many more?'

Dorothy Whamond

Historic Voyage

Those sudden changes, so ghostly stunning,
sprayed overall in virgin snow white.
To become a seafaring hospital,
virtually overnight.
New charters commissioned;
giving rules about wars
from officers pedantic,
who sometimes whispered
'Destination Falklands,' or
'Full steam ahead to the far Atlantic.'
Aboard were soldiers, arms and medics,
plus barely a normal enlisted crew.
In service already was the gallant Canberra,
as outward bound steamed the gracious QE2.

Normally she knew of affluence in the sun,
now sensed winter; morality without gain.
Wishing only to help those suffering
this forced benign, indissoluble campaign.
After brief bulletins came agonising silence.
Until they fought free from these hostilities.
Victory was announced with grateful splendour,
we then heard of casualties, losses or survivors
before the Argentinians decided to surrender.

Awaiting with excitement for the liners return,
thousands lined the Solent in eager expectation;
tears of emotion freely overflowing.
Loved ones and family united by exaltation,
as brass bands carried upon soft winds blowing.
Aboard the liners stood soldiers, medics and crew;
finally homeward bound, on the Canberra or QE2.

Geoff Ricketts

Christmas 1982

Shall we now celebrate the wondrous birth
When men forget the message *Peace on Earth*?
How can we after carnage and bloodshed
Still worship at the lowly manger bed!

In Northern Ireland, in religion's name
Man murders fellow man. How can this shame
Concord with what true Christians should believe,
How can they, then, God's mercy still receive.

In Poland Solidarity was crushed,
Aggression in Afghanistan is hushed,
So that the nations of the world forget
Those nations fighting for their freedom yet.

The name Beirut brings horror to the mind,
Nail bombs in London's parks have underlined
The brutal callous forces that have made
The towns and cities of the world afraid.

The stable is forgotten, and the song
Of angels from the earth has vanished long.
When con men and the muggers rule the earth
How can we celebrate with joy and mirth?

How long can God's forgiveness still prevail,
Is man for ever now without the pale
Of that redemption promised by Christ's birth
When evil men have shattered *Peace on Earth*!

Milly Blane

Thro' '85

Life in Britain thro' '85 - a time when you struggle to stay alive
With riots an' looting, fire an' strife
Not the place for the peaceful life

The fighting an' fury, no way to avoid - obvious links of the
vast unemployed
The homeless, the desperate, no easing the pain
Of constantly askin' for social again

Housebreaking, mugging, violence an' crime are the roots
and foundations of this land of mine
Gone is the sharing that we used to know
In so short a time how could we sink so low?

The spirit is missing that there used to be, the helping and caring
that we used to see
The ideals and values that we used to shout
Of freeing each other from worry and doubt

The old feel neglected - more trouble than worth - the Biblical
meek to inherit the Earth
Love's too much trouble an' cares in decline
We keep to ourselves for most of the time

The sick getting sicker, there is no respite, as services dwindle,
no end is in sight
There seems no sure answer to this feeling of rage
There must be a way in this day and age

The youth of our country are deep in despair; are we facing
the problem; do we really care?
For the young untrained future - a million or more
We should get a grip with this festering sore

No money invested in home industries is causing the closures
in our factories
The rich getting richer; the poor can't compete
With the vast wealth of the so-called *elite*

Rates, rents and taxes are taking their toll, as stocks and resources
are dwindling low
The government's panicked and passing new laws
Completely dumfounded, not knowing the cause

They lack all the answers to the social disease
They lack the solution to the obscenities
Of unemployed millions of the *left* or the *right*
Is there an end to our spiralling plight . . . ?

Norman Whittle

Time for the Eighties

Once upon a decade,
When Thatcherism governed our privatised land;
Adam and the Ants were a chart topping band.
Rubik's cube challenged, while trivial knowledge was pursued.
Diet coke, vegetarianism and restaurants for fast food.
Video, compact discs, computers and breakfast TV,
Eastenders versus Neighbours and the much loved film, ET.
Ice dance sporting excellence from Jayne Torville and Chris Dean.
IRA bomb attacks; heartless, cruel and mean.
Ra-ra skirts, double dutch, rap and microwave.
Environmentalists unite - the ozone layer they must save.
British and Argentinean conflict in the Falkland Islands' war.
Aerobics boom, bar-code, pin machines and more . . .
Wrestling winds of '87, destroying many beautiful trees.
Combined examination replaced O levels and CSE's.
Patriotic Britons celebrate the wedding of Charles and Di.
Horrific Lockerbie disaster; we pray, we cry and wonder why?
Shergar the horse was stolen and never found.
Acid house in night-clubs - late eighties regular sound.
Colder than the South Pole, temperatures plummet and freeze.
Nation-wide awareness of AIDS, the killer disease.
Our heritage, our history, Hampton Court goes up in smoke.
Unemployment multiplies and millions left broke.
Bonce boppers, robotics, the energetic breakdance,
Beauty treatments, hairstyles and fashions to enhance.
Ten years over. Another decade full of mystery
To ponder and reflect upon when the nineties are history!

Jacqui Fairley

Goodbye to the Eighties

Goodbye, goodbye,
It's goodbye again
To the *happy ever afters*
Told of happy men;
No there's no silver lining
Sewn into the sky,
Just a faded smile
Waving a slow goodbye.

Carl Deighton

Ruined

We thought we lived
Like Kings back then
Never knew
What it was all about
Only fooling ourselves
Now look what has happened
To your world
And to mine
Seems back then
Our tears were wasted
By the things that had been done
Now I look back
And the after taste
Is bitter in my mouth

We thought we were so clever
We'd seen it all
And all this time
We thought
We didn't have to learn anymore
About the world in our hands
Used and abused
Here we stand
Meeting our needs
Satisfying all our wants
Burning money
Like only we knew how
And the after taste
Is always bitter in my mouth.

Grant Imlach

The World Dies on My Say - So

Oh, so you want to save the world?,
Well I guess that's an admirable occupation.
Now you've seen the pictures of socially battered bunnies
And dolphins forced squealing into tins,
I suppose you really had to do something.

Oh, so you've stopped drinking, loving and breathing,
Well I wonder what the next step could be?
And now you want me to follow your shining example,
Although you know I would never hug a tree, at least not deliberately.

Oh, so you'll teach again, despite the warnings -
Well don't you remember when you were showered with stones
And you made that extravagant comparison?

Oh, so you want to be a Jedi Knight?
Well I understand you've been under some pressure.

Oh, so you want to save the world?

Gareth Lewis

Last Glass of Wine

I looked at the eighties
Like a new summer wine
When I tasted abroad for the very first time
In a decade strewn with complete Tory rule
We were skipping through brochures or basking by a pool

Sitting in a bar
In Puerto-De-La-Cruz
The papers spoke of mourning when Bill Shankly passed away
And though I was reared in the colour of blue
Brought a tear to my eye when I read them that day

From the shores of Britannia
An Armada did sail
To recapture the Falklands from a foreign betrayal
The Junta screamed innocence losing face in the sun
With a people still haunted by Eva Peron

For Heysel and Hillborough
I whispered a prayer
Passing tributes of thousand with invisible words
San Francisco teased the devil his reprimand was due
An earth fault yawned and a prophesy came true

Wars rained daily
Like a weather report
With the near death of Parliament in a holiday resort
The Soviets were slipping from their Bolshevik past
With her satellite countries wanting freedom in mass

It's strange how I pictured
Lost visions and prayers
And back door democracies now standing in line
'Twas just memorabilia sifting thoughts in my mind
Saying farewell to the eighties with my last glass of wine.

David Bridgwater

Epitaph of a City

Oh dirty city why do you blame?
Unemployment for your streets of shame

Graffiti sprayed at dead of night
It really is a sickening sight

Buildings damaged, windows smashed
Old people mugged, their faces slashed

Trees uprooted signs torn down
This really is a sorry town

Litter is casually dropped in the street
Remember the park? Where once stood *our seat*

The council spends money, alas it's in vain
No sooner repaired, then it's broken again

The telephone kiosk lasted a day
We've got to tell them, that it's not the way

The sickening idea they've got to destroy
Everything that's pleasing to see

Oh city of shame as the years go by
No more can you ever, hold your head high

Visitors came and your praises sung loud
Now your grim streets are masked with a shroud

Oh city you once were a joy to behold
Now you bear the scars of the young and the old

Us old ones we fought for the right to be free
And to live out our lives in peace

We look to the skies with hope in our eyes
Praying this destruction will cease

Colin Mills

Whatever Happened to Global Warming?

Towards the end of the eighties
global warming was predicted,
hot sunny days and endless drought,
so water was restricted.

But can I take the brick out of the loo now mum?
It's raining cats and dogs?
The lawn's knee deep in water,
large slugs, toadstools and frogs.

I know that the ozone layer
holds worries for us all
but there's rain pouring through the ceiling
into a bucket in the hall.

Is it really still necessary
to have one's hot bath with a friend?
She always hangs on to the soap
and makes me sit at the tap end.

The addition of an *Oxo*
to dirty water in the sink,
doesn't make it a less disgusting soup
whatever you may think.

To use it to wash the dog
is a practise most unwise,
as whenever he's taken for a walk,
he's followed by the flies.

Well I'm off to the timber yard
before it gets too dark,
to buy some nails and sturdy planks
with which to build an Ark.

Pauline Brennan

Refugees From the Sixties

(The fourth of May is Beatles Day)

Were the Sixties ever here?
You wouldn't know unless you see
Out on the street; a refugee.
And why it is that people leer
With sly innuendo?

All you need is love. Isn't it true?
Outlaw war and that means you.
What is money? What is it for?
Enough for me; enough for the poor?
Share the world and all its wealth.
Ban the bomb and keep your health.
All the freedom to educate.
To go back to school or vegetate.
Jobs galore to change about.
GCE's to give you clout.
Take your place at university.
Study to be an apothecary.
The Doc has a pill for every ill.
Computers and robots will pay the bill.
Comfortable from cradle to grave.
Nothing on earth for man to crave.

They look so sad and out of touch.
With their floating hair in need of a brush.
The embroidered top. The tattered trews.
As they slowly now give out their news.
'Man,' they say, 'We had it all
Where has it gone? Put out a call.'
And who would argue? They were right!
It just got mangled in the night.

Gladys Birmingham

Where Now - in the Eighties?

Where in this world is there *Quiet and Peace,*
Tranquillity and harmony - rare?
Where can I find that *Silent Hour* -
For *Meditation, reflection and prayer?*

Where now - the joy - bringing *instant lift* -
Which lingers, and brightens the day?
How oft' do we find - *The contented child* -
With *little* - yet *Happy at Play*?

What happened to *Trust and Constancy*?
To marriage *till Death* - us do part?
To love - which endures for a *lifetime*?
That Pledge Sincere - from deep, in the heart?

What has happened to *family ethics*,
Together *Mother and Father* - to guide?
Where now *Discipline - Respect and Affection* -
To *Honesty, and to Pride*?

Children will e'er - *Emulate Example* -
Of those - *Upright*, lawful and strong;
But copy also - *Corruption and Immorality* -
Too much in evidence, for too long!

Time - should be *spent* with children each day,
They need - *Honest Values and Faith* -
A future devoid of *Vice and Crime*,
Whilst - *Greed and Selfishness* - gives way to Grace!

There must be a way to return to *Standards*
Of *Christian Caring* - for those *Big and Small*,
And *The Unity* - which filled the *Soul with its strength*,
Spreading warmth, and well being to all!

Gertrude Parsons

After Hillsborough

The day dawns bright but shadows fill the morning
Oh why, oh why did no-one heed the warning?
Time after time as young lives are lost
Questions are asked and we have to count the cost.

Young men and old, all some mother's son,
Our loved ones we cherished each and every one.
Grim faced we stand and silent the town
Sleepless the night passed, morning wears a frown.

The shame and the pity wring my heart with pain
Oh why in this world, it seems quite insane?
The dead and the injured, what's it all about?
Flowers fill the terrace where a young life was crushed out.

Silent the morning and grim faced the town
No birds sing as people gather round
In pubs and in churches where mates are to be found
But faces are missing, others get the round.

Glasses are raised but voices are hushed
Here's to the old man, one who was crushed.
Cheers to the team and to days long gone,
Shadows in the morning as the sun shines on.

Jean Carroll

The Grabbing 1980's

Some remember the '80's with fondest memories
Others the memories are painful, full of treachery,
I look back at the Champagne yuppies with dismay,
Driving their BMW's and Porsches au fait,
There are the Lager louts drunk with thuggery,
A couldn't care less generation, full of skulduggery,
There was the Iron Lady that wouldn't give way,
On privatisation, VAT and her political swordplay
Wielded against world affairs, with hammered iron,
Going down in history as a real paragon?

I remember the rising cardboard city in London
Precious souls thrown on the scrapheap cauldron,
There was rising crime and single mums on the dole,
Rich getting richer, poor going down the plug hole,
House prices went through the roof, inflation rose,
Unemployment escalated and shops closed.
House repossessions, families went into bed and breakfast,
Hopes dashed, economic recession forecast,
Will our Bulldog spirit get us through tough times?
We must have a vision and conquer juvenile crime.

David Dawrant

Silver Wedding

(6th August 1960 - '85)

On an August day
We signed the line
To say
We would stay true.

In the year six-o
We made a vow
To go
Together life through.

Twenty-five years on,
Through stormy waves
Upon
The marriage sea.

Now - our silver year,
We'll celebrate
My dear,
Happy Anniversary

Jean Stewart

North East 1988

Dread dead dole days -
pointless - hopeless -
          but
Saturday night *lives.*

Teenage tarts,
T-shirts stretched tight
over taunting tits
seduce hard men
in smoke filled wine bars -
dispense cheap thrills -
AID life
to real death.

Doreen Dean

Of Mary Poppins and Toffee Apples

Cut off denims and white crop tops,
Pop music comforting in its banality
And a world that ended outside the playground.

A childhood bathed in sunlight
With scent of warmth and safety,
And a life without bus passes and Formica.

No bells, no forms, no ambitions;
No vote and no guilt.
A world of immortality and guarantees.

The eighties protected my childhood
With a motherly tenderness now hazed
In euphoric reflection;
They were as round as the nineties are jagged.

Emma Brockes

Dirt and Dust

Oh city of dirt and dust,
Oh painted child of blood tears crying in the gutter,
a river of your poverty's rust.
Broken down bodies pleading for coins,
stunted economic growth, no fertile baby
from the Prime Ministers loins.
Fingers of a loving couple entwine, endearments mutter
in secret breath, break away
to end the tender kiss of a last day.
To fight for his country like a man
the lad went to war the torpedoes ran.
His remains came back in a wooden box;
her souvenir a piece of his burnt, shrivelled up lock.
The striking miner's wives with placards lead
Give us some bread
to save our jobs
Oh hungry are the starving mobs
that sacrifice themselves in the name of society
for work and equality.

Julie Mears

Happy Days

The Eighties left a legacy
Of millions on the dole
Trust a Tory government
To get you in a hole!

Ms Thatcher did her utmost
But the thing that she did best
Was to give *Joe Soap* inflation
Whilst she *feathered* her own nest!

We still struggle with inflation
High prices, jobs are few
Is there anybody left out there
With an optimistic view?

And the argument that's given
Is that each political party is the same
But if you can recollect the Eighties
Then you'll know who is to blame!

Jean Boon

World in Action

The bank rate's up, mortgages rise,
The purse tightens, the Government lies,
Generals want guns, doctors beds,
While the air we breathe fills with lead.
Communists become capitalists, Fascists reformers,
Eastern Europeans carrying torches,
Transmittable diseases ravage the land,
We mustn't eat food that hasn't been canned.
Our basic industry is on the decline,
No hope for the miners down the mine,
Families split up because of divorce,
While the Americans have a show of force.
Students are crushed in Tiananmen Square,
Sellafield has another nuclear scare,
The city suffers from insider dealing,
While a nine year old is arrested for stealing.
Third world governments beg for food,
While our own tells us that greed is good.
Sea levels rise, the ice caps are melting,
Rivers polluted by aluminium smelting,
Fleet Street editors make the front page,
Sleeping with girls less than half their age.
In this world filled with so much sorrow,
There must be hope for a better tomorrow.

Bruce W Duthie

The Changes in Time

I often sat and wondered why,
I used to see my mother cry,
I was far too young to understand,
what was happening to the land.

But as I grew I saw the way,
things had changed since yesterday,
and I began to understand,
what was happening to the land.

Doors once open, now shut tight,
muggers and burglars, giving old folk a fright,
so maybe now you'll understand,
what is happening to the land.

There are conmen at the door,
stealing money and much more,
so can you try and understand,
what is happening to the land.

And as my children sleep tonight,
with doors and windows all locked tight,
I have learnt to understand,
what is happening to the land.

So when my children ask me why,
they have seen me sit and cry,
they're still too young to understand,
what is happening to the land.

Diane Higgins

Radio Days

Those radio days.
Jingles jangled like a sixties revival,
And everything was *fab!*

The characters on our hospital radio station,
Were either wildly eccentric or simply amazing.
Corny jokes and absurd clichés,

We all thought one day, we were going to be DJ's.
While me and my friends caused mayhem on the air,
Experimenting, inventing, creating new ways of presenting,
If it didn't work, we didn't care!

We turned off the power, turned some knobs, flicked some switches,
Playing tricks on confused DJ's, we rolled around in stitches!
We were told we would get nowhere, we tainted the Status Quo,
But a few of those yesterday's rebels, now have shows on local radio.

Darren Powell

Living My Teens in the Eighties

Duran Duran,
Michael Jackson,
and Wham!
Blue eye liner,
Red lipstick,
and jeans.

School homework,
School discos,
School dinners,
Beans and chips.

Rounders,
Cross Country,
Volley Ball,
and sherbet dips.

Casuals
and Mods,
Rebels,
and Bods.

Now memories to me,
Thank God it's '93!

Eve Chapman

A Band Aid Made it Better

We seemed to lurch from stepping stone to stepping stone,
Slip sliding our way through a disaster zone
Of enormous magnitude.
In Africa, people were dying of starvation.
The whole Etheopean nation
Waited for it in the stunted, Ogaden, brushwood.
We sailed away to fight in a far off, Falkland's war,
While The Jam sang *War*! What is it good for?
Absolutely nothing!
Maybe more people should have learned to sing
That, instead of Land Of Hope and Glory.
The Lady would have had to be for turning then.
Chuck married Di. That turned out to be a future disaster story.
The Exon Valdes poured its crude oil cargo over the seas
Transforming them into a deadly, cloying, quagmire.
Piper Alpha roared in an exploding ball of fire.
At Hillsborough, people were compressed against a chain link pen.
We watched them being asphyxiated on national TV.
The Ayatollah Hominee put out a contract on Salman Rushdee.
The miners struck. Riot police struck back.
AIDS and HIV laid in wait to bushwhack
Gays and the innocent, bystanding, haemophiliac.
The Eighties was not my favourite decade.
It's one redeeming feature was Bob Geldof's Band Aid.

Jan Ferrierr

Living in the Eighties

I had trials and tribulations like most people do,
But living through the eighties always brought something new,
It certainly was a decade of such dramatic change,
It was very rewarding with the more wisdom I gained,
I gather inspirations from travelling Life's Highway,
And hope people enjoy reading about what I have to say,
This was a joyous time I feel,
The joy of living brought that special appeal.
An all new era started for me,
A new marriage and child to expand the family,
A time of travel from plain to plain,
All over England and back again,
Exploring every corner lots of places to pursue,
Broadening my horizons, always finding somewhere new,
My poems were an inspiration I was lucky on the way,
People read my poetry brightening up my day . . .

Denise Frost

Death Cry of a Decade

Look at your face -
rainbow stained and lapped
by stiffly sprayed hair.
Day-glow plastic jewellery
matches your petty foolery
as the dawning of an end
to your cheap leisure pleasure
begins to awake in the eyes of your nation.
Choose carefully, my dear:
you never know where they've been,
even less of what they've seen.
Yet you are no angelic creation,
or at least you aren't anymore,
flushing your mortality
down the U-bend of this decade.
Stay in with safety and a well leafed TV guide,
it's cold and increasingly violent outside;
and as another TV hero is shamed by death,
thank common sense for teaching this drastic lesson
in time to save your life.

Simone Eade